KV-194-681

Getting Promoted

Other Classmates:

2nd Series

Successful Subject Co-ordination – Christine Farmery
Parent Partnership in the Early Years –
Damien Fitzgerald
Playing Outdoors in the Early Years – Ros Garrick
Assemblies Made Easy – Victoria Kidwell
Homework – Victoria Kidwell
ICT in the Early Years – Mark O'Hara
Creating Positive Classrooms – Mike Ollerton
Getting Organized – Angela Thody and
Derek Bowden
Physical Development in the Early Years –
Lynda Woodfield

1st Series

Lesson Planning – Graham Butt
Managing Your Classroom – Gererd Dixie
Teacher's Guide to Protecting Children – Janet Kay
Tips for Trips – Andy Leeder
Stress Busting – Michael Papworth
Every Minute Counts – Michael Papworth
Teaching Poetry – Fred Sedgwick
Running Your Tutor Group – Ian Startup
Involving Parents – Julian Stern
Marking and Assessment – Howard Tanner

Getting Promoted

Tom Miller

continuum
LONDON • NEW YORK

Continuum

The Tower Building
11 York Road
London SE1 7NX

15 East 26th Street
New York
NY 10010

British Library Cataloguing-in-Publication Data
A catalogue record for this book is available from the British Library.

ISBN 0–8264–7311–3 (paperback)

Typeset by BookEns Ltd, Royston, Herts.
Printed and bound in Great Britain by
Antony Rowe Ltd, Chippenham, Wiltshire

For Katy
With thanks to David Brent
for the quoted wisdom

So I was in my car, and I was driving along, and my boss rang up, and he said, 'You've been promoted.' And I swerved. And then he rang up a second time and said, 'You've been promoted again.' And I swerved again. He rang up a third time and said, 'You're managing director.' And I went into a tree. And a policeman came up and said 'What happened to you?' And I said, 'I careered off the road.'

Contents

Contents

Preface

There has never been a better time to get promoted in teaching. The lack of suitable candidates and the imminent retirement of many senior staff mean that the teaching labour market is ripe for you to make quick and relatively easy progression in your career. Many head teachers are desparate for competent, eager staff who are prepared to work hard for them.

The tricky bit is that the pool of people in a similar position to you is quite small and very focused on getting the right promotion. This book aims to give you a head start so that you are the best prepared candidate and therefore the most likely to be successful.

I have tried to write a guidebook for obtaining promotion, and so it is designed to be read from start to finish before you start applying, then to be dipped into for refreshment as you go through the process.

1

Why Get Promoted?

> *Eagles may soar high, but weasels don't get sucked into jet engines.*

Before doing anything about getting promoted consider what it involves and why you are doing it. There are lots of very good fundamental reasons to apply for more responsibility – but there are some poor ones too. Let's examine the good ones first.

Job satisfaction
Forty years as a classroom teacher is a long time and you might find the prospect of your job never really changing in that time quite dispiriting and demotivating, if not downright horrific. Terms like 'challenge' and 'change' will be watchwords for future thinking.

Responsibility
An idea much cited by aspiring teachers. However, if you look at the work your current line manager is doing and think it looks like no fun at all, then perhaps promotion is not for you.

Wanting to make changes
This is the fun and challenging aspect of leadership for me. It overlaps the previous ideas – but consider

the connotations. Nobody wants the hassle inherent in promotion; what people want is the ability to shape their own future and then to test their ideas to see if they work.

External circumstances
This is a relatively safe reason to give a current or prospective head teacher. Nobody can help your partner being transferred, so use it as good secondary justification. It isn't a reason for promotion in itself but it opens the door well.

There are also some very valid reasons that it might not be so wise to mention in your covering letter!

Money
The number one reason most people want promotion is to increase their personal income. To deny this would be difficult for most but it is the great unspoken truth. Teachers are so determined to be seen as altruistic, caring people that to appear concerned with money seems crass. This brings up a common theme in this book; playing the game. The people with the power to employ you got there by playing by the unwritten rules. Unfortunately, until you are in a similar position, you must abide by them too. (By then you might either realize why these rules exist or be so bitter you want everyone else to suffer like you did!)

The point of all this is, while the system is designed to use money to encourage and reward, you cannot admit it. So have a story worked out in advance.

Moving schools

Many people use promotion as a vehicle to extricate themselves from a situation they no longer want to be in. This is of course completely understandable but needs great care. The precautions you must take depend upon your situation but always, always be positive no matter how much it sticks in your throat.

Every situation has positives. Working for a rotten head teacher or inept faculty manager shows you how not to do it when you get to their position. And do not worry about them preventing you from leaving. Any recruiting head teacher worth their salt will spot the signs straight away and be even more eager to meet you.

To be with your partner

It is not up to me to judge whether this is a good idea or not, but be very careful how this is approached. On the one hand it gives you a very good perspective about a school, on the other the institution will dominate your life. Better to concentrate on the prospects the position will give you. One thing I am very happy to comment on is the wisdom of getting promoted to head the department of your partner/ wife/boyfriend. Don't. *Ever!*

Before you have decided that promotion is the right thing for you a lot of thinking is required. You may have the motivation but is it somewhere you want to go?

There are many pros and cons to climbing the pay scale. A minor point on the positive side of becoming a line manager is the higher profile you will have in school. A bizarre aspect of promotion is that most kids respect the (assumed) fact that you have been selected by the head teacher through a rigorous merit-based process. Consequently, you are listened to a bit more and being told off by you is a bit more serious. Weird but true.

Another little talked about aspect of promotion is that you will feel better about yourself. People trust you and have selected you above others to do an important job. I would not list rampant egomania as a valued personality trait, but having status is a nice feeling. Accepting the idea of job satisfaction brings into focus other aspects of career progression. The range of tasks you are expected to do and the experiences you gain from them increase greatly. To some extent you can now pick and choose which you complete and delegate the others, but in (good) practice this is seldom the case.

It might seem a little odd in a book written to improve your prospects of promotion to talk about the downsides and why you must be sure you want it, but I have seen too many people stuck in posts they are not suitable for, don't enjoy and in which they let their colleagues down. Look around your school and you might see them. Good teachers who hate their role are there because they need that extra bit of cash in order to pay the mortgage/university fees/green fees/bar tab. No matter where you are now in your life please do not get caught in this trap. In the modern world of education there is no real excuse to stay unhappy. There are plenty of opportunities, such as AST and overseas schools, and with LEAs, publishers and exam boards.

The reasons that middle managers become so defeated are many and numerous. Primarily it is workload. While you may have less teaching and marking there are so many additional demands on your time that you will scarcely notice. On top of this you are stuck between your department and your senior management team. Many middle managers complain of a sense of impotence; overloaded by short-term demands by their teachers and by initiatives from SMT. It is why most heads and inspectors acknowledge that a school fails or succeeds on the competence of its middle managers.

Negative stuff, but take the time to speak with somebody you trust about whether it is all going to be worth it. You will put your heart and soul into your new job and you must be prepared for the ups and downs.

Presuming that you are still reading, what must now follow is a process of self-examination. Look around your current school and identify the one or two managers you admire and the one or two you think are the worst. These latter two are not without qualities; they are above you so they must have done something right! A hard lesson of management all must learn is that everybody has strengths and no-one is without faults. The crucial thing to do is recognize them and adapt your own practice. It is not your job to be original; rather it is your duty to be as effective as possible.

Having selected your positive and negative 'role models', think about what it is that made you name them. It can be anything, because if it attracted your attention it will attract other people's too. Then think of the opposite list. What is it that this manager does well despite all the criticism he gets? Everybody thinks she is great but what does she not do well? The chances are that if she is as good as you think then they will have informally done the same process and vice versa! Nobody expects you to be perfect but if you know what your strengths are then you are best placed to use them at every opportunity.

A word of warning though: asking around can lead to all sorts of issues. A school is a very insular place and there is a great possibility that any opinion has a 'back story'. Beware of bias, even from those you trust or who don't even know they are distorting the truth.

Once you have your list of qualities, good and bad, set about identifying the ones you have, the ones you wish to keep, the ones to develop, the ones to learn and the ones to avoid. Be reasonable, you cannot expect to change over night but the key question is:

What sort of manager do I want to be?

The fundamentals that this breaks down into are, of course, very specific to the individual, but may include the obvious decisions like pastoral or academic and the more esoteric such as facilitator or leader.

This is why the analysis of other leaders recommended earlier is so useful. It is up to you to make the decision about what sort of manager you want to be, but how to do it is often best learnt through observation.

After this first huge step of setting your sights on an ideology to take forward, the next thing to do is to start to accumulate the experiences to back up your ambitions.

Top Tips 1

1. Know why you want to be promoted.

2. Be sure that promotion is for you.

3. Make sure there is the space in your life to be more involved with school.

4. Know in yourself what qualities make a good manager.

5. It is just as important to recognize what makes a bad manager.

2

Building the Foundations for Promotion

What does a squirrel do in the summer? It buries nuts. Why? Because then in winter time he's got something to eat and he won't die. So, collecting nuts in the summer is worthwhile work. Every task you do at work think, would a squirrel do that? Think squirrels. Think nuts.

Once you have established that promotion is something that you really want, the hard work starts.

Your 'mission' now is to carry out your duties while building up the evidence to prove what a great appointment you would be. What follows is how to use common situations to your advantage, but please remember that every day contains a chance to impress. Head teachers take great store in the references that they write for each other and often ring schools if they have a local application. On top of that, the staff at your school might be rung up by a friend who teaches where you have applied and asked for a snapshot of what you are like. You have to convince all day every day. A tough assignment, but think of the cash/kudos/not having to go your current school again!

Before you embark on this difficult mission take the

time to consider what Heads are looking for when appointing somebody to their first middle management position. Top of their list must be that you will not cause them any problems, followed by, in no particular order: you will improve exam results; you can get on with people; you will improve the department/year group; and you will deal with problems. The challenge is how to use your unique, personal talents to be who they want. Head teachers are fantastically busy people so the last thing they want is for a new appointment to generate even more for them to do. You will of course make them more work, more of which later, but it is the perception that is all important. So take the time to build a portfolio of evidence that proves you are all these things and more.

Teaching

The most appropriate place to start impressing is in your own classroom and for all the advice that follows never lose sight of this. Your reference will be written primarily on your practice so do everything you can to be as effective as possible and then subtlety let everyone know about it. Remember that teachers do not find egotism a very attractive trait. Make the walls attractive, get the students on your side, take a trip and put it into the newsletter, show up at the awards evening you don't want to go to. What would impress you? How do you recognize a good teacher as you walk around the school? Use their ideas: flattery is the sincerest form after all.

Your tutor group

In most secondary schools, all middle managers will be expected to have a tutor group, so take the time to learn how to manage one well. Tutoring a form is unjustly overlooked considering it offers such significant opportunities for the ambitious.

For prospective pastoral leaders these are obvious. Show that you can manage this small group effectively of course, but try to expand your role. Mentor individuals, experiment with activities in tutor time and evolve strategies for dealing with parents to build your evidence base. Anecdotal evidence will be asked for at interview so any experience becomes valid. Be very careful to involve your head of year at the appropriate times however. You have to demonstrate that you are, above all else, a safe pair of hands and part of that is knowing when to pass problems up the chain. By all means be active and, for instance, get parents in to talk over problems – but know your limits!

For prospective subject leaders the benefits of knowing how to run a form group are less obvious but still very real. At the most cynical, your form will not be such a distraction when you get a new job, but this is the wrong way to approach it. Running a form allows you a (relatively) low-pressure job that raises your profile. Kids talk to each other and heads talk to kids, so do a good job. It isn't about being popular, it is about being effective. It is easily argued that the most ambitious subject leaders have to be good form tutors because it is only in this aspect that most will develop the pastoral skills necessary later in their career.

Getting Promoted

Letting people know what an active form tutor you are is not difficult. The hard bit is demonstrating that you are a good one too. Think about what your school perceives as ideal qualities for a tutor. Solve problems that your form creates and tell the affected staff what you have done. Chase up everything you perceive as important, inform staff of potential problems. Being proactive is the key to good form tutoring so engender a team spirit within your form. If things blow up get them to write a report of what happened. This gives a powerful insight into the group's dynamics and points out the troublemakers from a new angle without the preconceptions of staff. Learn how the kids in your form behave under pressure so that you can predict their reactions to stressful situations and fight their corner when you think it is appropriate. There are many lessons to learn about handling students in form tutoring, so give the role the attention it deserves.

Meetings

Of all the occasions and events you will participate in, meetings have the greatest potential for pitfalls and pratfalls. There are so many unspoken rules in any given institution that care must be exercised at every opportunity.

In your next meeting, make a list of the stereotypes that you have at your school. There is bound to be a selection from the time-honoured list of clichés: bore; wordy bore; obstructive, wordy bore; only-out-for-himself bore; points-scoring bore; that guy who never says anything in an attempt to get home sooner; the list goes on and on.

I hate meetings and I haven't even reached the lowest point of any meeting, the dregs of the dregs; the person who thinks that by repeating everything that has just been said they will look clever.

No, there is a worse category. Those people who have an anecdote which is inappropriate and unhelpful to the situation at hand. These people have the ability to warp your perception of time so that the designated finish time actually seems to get further away as they talk.

Ranting away like this has given me real clarity. The worst, without doubt, person in a meeting is the compulsory contributor. Whatever the subject and however tenuous their link to it they simply have to say something. Pavlovian in the extreme, these people look forward to AOB in a meeting so they can voice concerns over either the most petty of details or over gigantic insolubles. Each point is made in a strangely smug and superior tone of voice that is supposed to convey a knowing greatness but in fact makes them sound smug and stupid. (I did make it clear earlier that I hate meetings.)

What are these people thinking? They are of course entitled to act as they wish, and I pity any one who lives with them, but imagine being the head teacher. He sits through more meetings than anyone else. How are you going to stand out from all this mediocrity and impress? Any response is very personal, of course, but there are several constants.

A difficult aspect when any issue of importance is being discussed is keeping quiet until what comes out has been thought through. Meetings are littered with the wreckage of not doing so. From naive through to inane, people cannot help themselves. Do not be the one who volunteers for the task that cannot be done successfully; producing an assessment policy to cover every subject, writing an equal opportunities document people will want to read or making your school a litter-free zone.

Likewise, do not live up to the stereotypes of education that rankle within the profession. Refuse to be that science teacher who asks for more technician support, the PE teacher after more marking time or the home economics teacher who interrupts forcibly whenever the subject is called cooking. Perceptions of subject staff are unavoidable in schools – how can everyone know everybody else? – and humorous stereotypes are sometimes based in fact, so be sensitive as to what your subject is notorious for. If you are not sure read the *Daily Mail* and ask your friends. They will delight in telling you.

Go with the flow. Teachers are supposed to be empathetic but too often it is only with children. If a meeting has dragged on for much longer than scheduled, be sensitive to the fact that many people will want to go home, don't prolong it. The burning issue you have can be resolved later. It is at emotional points like this that people will form their deep rooted and often irrational opinions of you. Who knows how they may come back to haunt you.

The opposite of this situation is when you chair a meeting. Do not underestimate the power the author of the agenda has. This cuts both ways: you can include and exclude what you want to focus on but you risk alienating people if you do not allow them a voice. Learn how to listen, or appear to listen, attentively. If I am ever found slumped at a conference table I am sure that the coroner will record 'Death by Anecdote' but the murderer will never know it (hopefully).

Be aware of the scale at which your meeting operates. Think what the chairperson is using the meeting for. Full staff meetings are very different to department meetings. One can be a public relations exercise; the other could be a focused attempt to make big steps with teaching and learning.

A final plea is that you take every precaution possible not to be that person who thinks they have something to say in every meeting. Of all the usual teacher characteristics, self-importance is the least likeable. Nobody listens after a while or cares about the arrangements for sharing protractors over the Spring Term. It is much better to be the few words strongly spoken type so that people actually take heed, or to work quietly and efficiently in the background.

Psychologists will no doubt love the next bit but my best way to survive a meeting is to substitute teacher jargon for various pieces of anatomy. The trick is not to snigger too much when you realize replacing pigeon hole with bum hole is the funniest thing you have heard. Ever.

Inspections

Ofsted offers a unique opportunity for you to have your abilities formally recognized by a trained observer who then writes them down. Everyone finds inspection difficult and stressful but head teachers find it more so than most. Consequently, someone who has proven themselves under the Ofsted spotlight is much more employable than someone who hasn't. Keep all the documentation, scour the final report for nuggets about you and put every effort into your lessons. Teaching will remain a significant part of role for the foreseeable future and you must be able to prove you are good at it.

Inspection within school offers a whole different set of problems. The key must be to know what is being looked for. Are you being checked for improvements since Ofsted or since the last school development plan? Will you be judged by in-house standards or by Ofsted standards? With this in mind, plan your conduct beforehand. Ask around and find out what certain staff look for and favour. Did one of them give an Inset session on a particular style of learning or in the last inspection did Ofsted criticize something in particular? Of course, you cannot change who you are, nor would it be realistic to suggest that you put on a completely fake persona, but small nods to preferred techniques will go down very well indeed.

The job for no money

With such a strong labour market for teachers at the moment the practice of giving people responsibilities for no reward is falling into decline. This is a shame because it offers ambitious staff a great chance to

shine without taking too many risks. It is recommended practice to take any opportunity offered to
you. These can vary but tend to be jobs like compiling
exam entries, running field trips or co-ordinating
induction sessions. There are few better ways to show
to a prospective employer that you are worthy and
able for promotion. But be careful. If you do not think
you could do a good job, politely say so. State how
flattered you feel to be asked and make sure that
whoever asks you understands why you have
declined. However, they would not ask if they thought
you were not up to it and saying no might be seen as
a lack of confidence.

Schools do have money for these posts now but
judge your situation before asking for it. You will make
a lot more from the subsequent promotion, so do not
risk losing it. A much more positive approach is to
carry out the task for a year then ask for a suitable
reward. Many heads use them as a cost-effective way
of retaining good staff; others recognize that people
need to be trained for further responsibilities. Typical
examples include Assistant head of year or department.

If you do accept a post make sure that you are
given the time to do it in. For instance, as a pastoral
deputy your time will disappear quickly. You cannot
do it if you have a tutor group as well. Similarly, as an
assistant to a department head you will acquire a lot
of time-consuming tasks. It is not unreasonable to ask
for some time to do these in, whatever your SMT
think.

Courses

Getting some courses on your application form says several things about you. It says that your head teacher has so much faith in your abilities that he is prepared to spend some money on you and that you are interested in this area. So, think carefully about the courses you write down. Too many on discipline suggests you are having problems. Too many on non-core activities (or the airy-fairy type) does not send out the right message either. Aim to get on one course a year that is focused on your areas of interest, be that pastoral or academic. Use them as evidence of your enthusiasm for your chosen future path.

When you do get lucky enough to be sent on a course make a note of it. The easiest way is to start a file on your computer. Every time you have a 'career-enhancing experience' make a note so that filling in the application forms of the future will be that much easier.

Extra-curricular activities

One simple statement here: head teachers love extra-curricular activities but will not pay for them. They love the breadth and depth they give to their curriculum, respect the effort and time you commit and appreciate all the benefits the children gain but they will not even consider giving you anything for them. If you are a PE teacher it is assumed that you will attend fixtures; language teachers by definition are expected to go on exchanges; humanities teachers are considered incomplete without field trips. Primary teachers have perhaps even more pressure put upon them to get the kids out and about. To not have done so raises eyebrows on application and puts you at a disadvantage to others who have done, so think of the positives as you ring the bus company and wait at the school gates for the last parent.

The staffroom

Any staffroom is by definition a funny place populated by funny people. While some of the rules are the stuff of folklore (the chair you mustn't sit in, the coffee fund you have to pay into to subsidize the person running it, etc.), there are others that you will see violated every time you are in there. Personally, I tend to avoid the place unless I know someone vaguely pleasant will be there.

One of the reasons is the constantly moaning teacher who thinks that talking in the staffroom is somehow confidential and, therefore, slagging off the head/deputy/cover teacher/you will be fine. What they are doing is shaping, however marginally, other people's opinions about the subject and themselves. It is impossible not to be influenced about the person being savaged by these people and the best way forward is to think the least of the perpetrator. That is the only fair way to deal with a difficult circumstance.

Another mistake I have witnessed in the staffroom is the overly laddish banter. Nob gags are great, but in the pub and not in here. Most teaching staff are middle aged and middle class. I tend to imagine they are all like my mum but of course the reality is that most resemble my granny. Any double entendre in a staff meeting or even putting things in people's pigeon holes must be done carefully and laughed at later. Your granny wouldn't like it and the chances are lots of important people won't either.

One part of staffroom life that deserves a mention is looking at the *TES* every Friday. Some schools have people queuing to read the jobs section. This is a bad sign and probably means you should join them. If you do not want to have your own copy delivered to your house then consider your position. Do you want people to know that you are looking or would it serve your purposes to keep it a secret? The fact that you are looking will be noticed and your senior staff could react by either being nicer to you or giving up on you! The way to deal with it is to think about your personal context and how SMT will react, but it is another great example of thinking ahead for repercussions.

Interacting with your immediate manager

Whatever you think of your current manager, it is vital that he or she thinks you think they are great. Remember that this person will write your reference and may well meet your prospective employers at courses and the like. So do not fall into the habit of slagging them off to other people but do not become a sycophant either. Your dealings with them should, at the very least, be professional and hopefully friendly. A tough job sometimes but worthwhile on all sorts of levels.

Share your seriousness about promotion with

them. They should see your ambitions as a positive; you are stating that you want to do more for them and any good subject leader will take full advantage of you. A bad one might need it pointing out!

This is the perennial problem for dynamic teachers like you. You have to let yourself be exploited in order to move up and some managers, bizarrely, won't take advantage. Whether it is founded in insecurity or ignorance it is an obstructive attitude. How else will you gain the experience to move on?

Now you are 'out and proud' about your wishes, you have someone fighting your corner for Inset money and thinking how they can use you so that you gain CV inches. Be prepared to do some really boring stuff and a lot of things nobody wants to do but put it all down as investment for the future. Well, try to!

Getting your head teacher on board

This is a tricky one. You know your head much better than I do but tread carefully. Ask your colleagues. Will your head see the advantages or will he only recognize the costs and problems of replacing you? If it is the former, talk to him and ask his advice. If it is the latter leave even more quickly!

Duty

Playground duty is another one of those terrible teacher activities that we have to do but there are things to gain from it. It is a great place to show how much the kids like/loathe/fear/respect/insert-desired-outcome you. You can have a good nose at other departments and other staff to see how they work and so copy as you see fit. It is a good place to raise students' awareness of you, although they do not always appreciate your attentions. Most of all it reinforces your public persona of someone who is a safe pair of hands so take care of things quietly and effectively, calling things to the attention of senior staff when you think they will want to know. Run your little corner well and people will notice.

Your advisory teacher

If you are lucky enough to have an advisory service in your LEA then make sure they know you. There is a chance that they may be on your interview panel soon and it wouldn't be a good move to upset them. External people like this carry a lot of clout and if they think you will make a good appointment to their subject in the area they will say so. Establish a relationship by ringing up for advice, asking about future vacancies and going on courses they run. If there is a county website then send in some materials for it. Obtain an understanding of what they think is good practice, trust their judgement and start to use it in your lessons.

In some areas the advisory service is very aware that it needs to be self-sustaining and will be very keen to help rising stars like you. In others, the market-forces mentality has still to take hold and you will have to be smarter at getting the best out of them.

Sports day

I have chosen this rather bizarre topic to illustrate that every occasion is an opportunity. At the next sports day look around. The staff will split into categories that are obvious and explicit and the same groups appear at every similar occasion: school photo, end of term assembly, fire practice …

There will be people who savour the time off and have a chat while drinking from their ever-present coffee mug. Others will stand around, to all intents and purposes sentient but oblivious to everything. Then there are the two groups you should find yourself in: one on general crowd control and the other carrying out a specific duty that they asked to be allocated earlier.

Both have advantages, both serve very useful functions and both are valid roles for you to fill. Heads like to see people being proactive, getting stuck in, and solving problems before they happen. Here is a great opportunity to show that this is what you are, a positive addition to the staff. And if the head notices then every one else will too. The key for most people is not to see these events as upheavals from routine but as fun times to show yourself in a better light. If you doubt the wisdom of thinking positively consider that you will have to endure 40 of them for a full pension!

Examining

A personal favourite of mine for improving every aspect of your career opportunities is working for an exam board. It can be tough to do at primary level, and perhaps not so relevant, but opportunities do now exist throughout all key stages and the benefits are innumerable. It is finding the time that is difficult and the reason why most people do not try it. Even prospective heads of year can use examining to help themselves because the first thing potential employers will look for is good quality teaching.

Many look on it as a failing of our exam system that a significant proportion of marks are won by exam technique, but whatever your feelings, face up to it as a fact. By putting yourself into the system you will gain a great insight into how it works. Consequently, you will become a more effective teacher, your exam results will improve and you are more employable.

Other fringe benefits include access to the training and the associated materials, a 'nice day out' and a nice sum of money to help tide over the summer holidays. It is quite fun to meet the top examiners too – but that is probably more to do with my out of control ego than anything else!

The Christmas party

I have left the most difficult situation until last because there is no easy advice to give. The last few pages have been about constructing the most convincing persona to fulfil your ambitions. Dependable, sensible, in control and trustworthy are by now all descriptors that people associate with you but the staff party is the most likely place to destroy it all.

I will discuss the hackneyed and clichéd advice

that you will receive in more detail later, but the weariest (and least helpful) of all of it is 'Just be yourself'. If this was the case then you would not have even heard of any ineffective managers nor would you be reading this book. Being yourself might be the last thing you should do!

You do not arrive in teaching fully formed. You have to adapt, learn new tricks and flex with situations. Good managers are shaped, not born. After any experience at all, you are not yourself. You do not go to see your prospective in-laws 'being yourself'. You do not try to do any conscious act as yourself. Every time you think about doing anything you are no longer yourself. One of the basics of good manners is not being yourself. So why be yourself in truly career-defining moments? Better still why risk all those moments while under the influence of the one thing that makes you yourself – alcohol?

Every one has different tolerances and different reactions to alcohol, but the results are often the same. The wrong comment at the wrong time, a lingering gaze over a member of the opposite sex, the horrible faux pas; they are all just symptoms of who you are after some booze. And it isn't a tipsy you that will get promotion. It certainly would not be a pissed me, however hilarious I think I am!

So do not go. Or, if it is rude not to go, drive. It is just too risky to go on the piss with senior people from school who you don't have as friends already. Trust me!

In summary, while it might seem scheming and calculating to manipulate your personal image to this extent, there really is no other option. I am not advocating a complete change of who you are. Rather more a gradual movement towards a more contemplative, professional and reflective way of doing things. Most other professions have worked this out and it is common sense. The aim now must be to use all this ground work to the best possible effect.

Top Tips 2

1. Impress at every opportunity.

2. Be proactive in building a range of experiences that show you as capable, useful and dynamic.

3. Do the basics of teaching really well.

4. Appreciate how you will be perceived by others every time you do anything at school and work at colouring that perception in your favour.

5. Share your ambitions with those that can help you.

6. Be prepared to do the unglamorous stuff.

7. Stay sober at the Christmas party!

3

Applying for Your First Management Post

Avoid employing unlucky people – throw half of the pile of CVs in the bin without reading them.

What follows is advice for any advertised post. The complexities of applying internally and externally are dealt with separately below.

Looking for your first management post

After a while you will have had enough of a taste to decide that promotion is something you really do want. You will be convinced that you are capable and that you are prepared to make the sacrifices.

The first step is to talk to your partner or family about what the future might hold. They have to be prepared for the time you are going to give to your career, and not them, as well as being willing to support you at crunch times. Middle management need not take up all of your time but it will take up more than you give now, and your family must come first. An unhappy manager is often an ineffective manager.

Sit down with them and decide how much

upheaval you are prepared to endure for the first step. The financial rewards are not that much greater so it might seem unwise to sell your house for a new job, but make a decision early on. When you have chosen a geographical area it is time to survey all the schools that it covers.

Start talking to people about which institutions you might want to aim for. PE teachers are a fantastic source of information because they visit other schools all the time for fixtures. Take the time to read Ofsted reports on the web to sort out desirables from undesirables. If you have an advisory teacher, who you will have buttered up earlier, ask about which schools would be good places to learn the ropes of middle management. The local press should however not be trusted as any sort of source of truth. In my local area one mediocre school's policy is to make sure they are in the local press every week to cultivate a fantastic image for themselves. It works too. They look great on paper but the exams results are never trumpeted quite so loudly as the new minibus sponsor.

A more reliable method to learn about a school needs a little planning. Without being creepy or arrested, park up outside a potential school and see how the kids act as they leave. If they take your wing mirrors off you might want to cross it off your list. If, however, the staff show themselves on duty, the kids leave in an orderly fashion with most of their uniform on and the bus drivers aren't armed then it is probably worth a further look. If you can't get there during the week have a look on a Saturday. Is the sports centre open and has it been vandalized? Are the local shops full of signs that say 'No school children'? Is the field knee-deep in litter? Remember to look for signs other than the obvious symptoms of difficult pupils. Does the school look well maintained? Is there money available for things other than security fences and CCTV?

It is very tempting to look for a school in difficult circumstances so that you look even better for turning it around. This is very, very difficult to do and I warn against it. There is a reason why these schools cannot get people to manage them; it is really difficult to succeed. It is far better for a first promotion to be somewhere you do not have to worry about survival so you have time to do the manager thing. There is plenty of time for helping these schools when you have some experience of what works and what doesn't.

When you have a series of schools you consider meet your needs, then it is time to scour the newspaper for advertisements. There is some debate about the validity of writing to schools expressing your interest. On the plus side they may have a vacancy coming up and ask you for interview. Much more likely is that they will keep your letter on file and let you know when an advertisement is published. But there are negatives too. Writing to heads gets them thinking about why you are so desperate to get out or gets them talking to your head and, if you haven't cleared it with them first, it could be perceived as rude or disloyal. Personally, I always think that if someone is keen enough to work at my school then they will make sure they see the advert.

Once the suitable job comes up

The instant that a job comes up that you think you want, applying for it must be your number one priority. Put off everything else otherwise you will not give it your best shot and it is imperative that you do so to get the best possible chance.

As soon as the advert is published you must ring up for the details but do not waste valuable time waiting for them to arrive before you start writing your letter. You must also now start to garner every opinion about the target institution. Ask your head and colleagues what it is like, ask if they have friends there you could talk to, ring the advisory team at the LEA and chat frankly about what you want and whether this school is the place to achieve it. Your head will have met most other local heads and therefore will be able to tell you whether you would fit in or not. Be warned that everyone who offers an opinion has a bias, deliberate or not. Try to sift a truth out from all the involved personalities so that your decisions and performance are the best they can be.

You will be given about two weeks to get your application in, so by the end of the first weekend your position should be: details asked for, anecdotal evidence about the place collected, Ofsted report downloaded and the web searched for articles on the school. It is worth examining the advert carefully. Many schools have a plethora of marks and awards of a bewildering range of validity. Make sure you know what each means and start to think ahead. What does each one signify?

'Investor in People' is a common inclusion on most

schools' headed paper, but it doesn't mean very much at all. In contrast, specialist school status must be responded to in your letter. Each mark must be considered for its merits with regard to whether you need to address it. It can be a good indication of the school's priorities but check that the current head was there when they were earnt. Knowing about these awards shows that you are serious enough about the job to have researched them.

The Ofsted report must be dissected in detail. The key areas for you as a middle manager are the whole-school strengths, your specialist area's report and the development plan at the end, but do not ignore any of it. Put yourself in the head's shoes. What will she want to see in a candidate? Which qualities will help the school address the shortcomings found by the inspectors? Which of these can you offer? The head will know the report like the back of her hand and, consciously or subconsciously, will respond to it. If you can fill the gaps in for her you are immediately ahead of the competition.

During the first week of the job being 'out there' the information pack will arrive. Spend a lot of time pulling it to pieces and analysing every component. Do not be too influenced by the stationery. There are plenty of good schools that spend the money on the kids rather than the embossed, posed, full-colour, gatefold sleeve and just as many bad schools who hide behind the embossed, posed, full-colour, gate-fold sleeve. There are a few pointers in there though.

Is there a picture of the head in the bumf? Experience informs that this is probably a bad thing if they are alone in their office and a good thing if they are in a classroom. Even if it isn't a true reflection at least it shows they have the sense to pretend. In these media savvy days I don't suppose that there are many heads pictured bollocking kids to tears, but staff would be queuing up to apply!

There are school brochures out there that cover the entire spectrum of quality. Some exude a quiet efficiency, others shout desperation. I have seen all sorts including Banda-produced notes, packs that include notes on every policy in the school and full-colour glossy brochures in which every photo was totally devoid of students. All very dodgy but do not make your decision purely on the strength of the details. There are perfectly legitimate reasons for any of them. (Except perhaps the student-less school. What sort of place cannot find a dozen kids who will dress smartly and behave for a few photos? Actually, I don't want to find out!) So use them to get a flavour rather than dump the idea altogether.

It does work the other way though. A good school will shine out of its paperwork. There will be a thorough job description indicating that the post has been thought out in depth. The paperwork will be functional not flash. The accompanying letter will be signed by the head and will arrive promptly, first class. A brief profile of the school will be there too and you will be able to read the pride the school takes in its students and their achievements. And it won't be run off a Banda machine.

The second weekend is the time to fill in the form and write your letter. There are many traditions it is difficult to ignore. A maximum of two sides of white A4 and the opening statement describing where you saw the advert is obligatory. Remember you want to be a safe pair of hands, a dependable teacher not a flash advertising executive, so orange paper and PowerPoint files are not the way forward. A decent pen shows a little bit of class. Remember that your audience (the head, the governor, a senior manager) are most likely to be a lot older than you are, so conform to their expectations.

My current school advertised recently for a science teacher and received several replies. In our local area, people to teach chemistry only need to be able stand unaided most of the time and know how to spell the chemical symbol for hydrogen. Yet still letters were discarded because the standard was so poor. It is a strong labour market at the moment but if you hand write your letter in biro only a very, very desperate school will want you for vacancies they have no realistic hope of filling.

Application forms

Before writing your letter, fill in your form. Or rather, fill in a photocopy of your form. Some schools have taken to stamping their application forms. This is a bit suspicious. It seems to be saying that knowing how to hand write a form is a skill you need in the modern workplace. See what I mean about the mindset being different because of age gaps. If I ever, God help me, become a head I promise I will send the form out on floppy disc or DNA or whatever is current at the time.

Anyway, once you have remembered how to write

in a colour other than red, practice each section. Be careful when it comes to the GCSE/O level section. A lot of the perception of the form is based on its presentation so do not sprawl across it all the different certificates you are so proud of. Recognize that they are way beneath you and write something like '10 GCSEs at grade C or above including Maths, English and your subject specialism'. They will not care about much else. A Levels are different however. Include all the subjects and the grades you achieved. And be prepared to answer the question 'I see you have an A level in Dance, would you be prepared to teach it here?' even if you are applying for Head of Food Technology.

Your degree is also important to specify. With graduate training schemes and the like, many people now have degrees in subjects that are not on the National Curriculum. You might think your American Studies degree is really useful, but show the reader explicitly how and why it is. There is often a space to let you write about the components of your qualification: use it to ram home the elements relevant to your subject.

There is always a box to write in your other interests. Strike a balance. Show that you are not a teaching machine and that you have a life but do not include so many that questions are asked about how you ever find the time to come to school. Try to include something that ties in with your prospective position but don't force it. By having out of school interests you are signalling that you are a real person, but remember your target audience. Graffiti artist, dynamic member of the Socialist Worker Party or vigorous user of recreational substances should probably not be included in the final draft. Also, do not fall in to the trap of making hobbies up to appear interesting. Instead, if you really have nothing to put, leave it blank. At interview, if asked, make a joke about how your social life is so run of the mill you were embarrassed to mention it. Lots of people go to the pub without being in CAMRA, just as most of us buy CDs without being a collector of rare Mid-West American buzz pop. Don't worry; it is not a major disaster.

Unlike the wrong referees. For all the work you will put in to your application the biggest deciding factor about whether you will get an interview is what your referees write. This is why you have put in all that work preparing the foundations for your promotion. Ask your referee before you nominate them and chat about what type of things they will include if asked. That way they might be prepared and send their reference that little bit more quickly. Check that they will write good things. If you know them really well ask to see the reference before it goes off but do not be surprised if they are a little coy about this. Teaching is still a profession that finds the whole idea of peer praise difficult, so be sensitive.

What you do if they write an unfair reference is much more difficult. If you do find out, I would favour asking them so that you are able to remedy their complaints but don't panic. I have seen quite a few examples of candidates who have a stinker written by their subject leader, but a glowing report from their head. These people get interviewed straight away. What is it that the head of department is so scared of losing? If you do get a bad reference, next time put the next manager up the line as your reference and give them a title that stretches the truth a little. Like i/c Languages Faculty or Deputy Head Teacher (Pastoral). There really isn't time for the school to fiddle about asking for more references and they will probably call you for interview anyway. It is also vital to speak to your head if you find out about a duff reference, particularly if it is at odds with his. It all comes down to their individual perceptions. If they are so small-minded that they do not want you to get on and make the most of your career they are simply confirming the validity of you leaving. Get out as soon as possible. Most reasonable head teachers faced with a bad or dodgy reference will ask you along and make a decision with their own judgement.

Another top tip a head teacher's secretary (you shall call her God!) told me is to include as many contact details as is practical. With short deadlines and teacher shortages, schools are often scurrying around to get enough interviewees to make it a valid process, so you not answering the phone does not help. They would never admit it but I bet sometimes they give up if people are tricky to contact. So give your mobile number and check your answer machine, leave contact numbers if you go away and sweet talk the secretaries to bring any faxes to your classroom. If you aren't at the interview you will not get the job.

CVs

Much of the advice above rings true for CVs too. One big advantage of being asked to include one is that you can decide what goes in and what gets forgotten. Use it to highlight the achievements you are most proud of and to disguise the things you are least proud of. Do not, however, distort the truth too much. Schools have the right to believe that what you write is true and are quite capable of sacking you if it is not. The other big advantage is that you can have a CV pre-prepared to save time on the letter of application.

The letter of application

Now that you have a very good idea about your new school it is time to sit down and write your letter. While there are some aspects that you can repeat in each letter the core text must be specially written for each school. There might not be major differences between two of your letters but that should be because of similarities between the institutions rather than your letters being identikit. This not only avoids embarrassing mistakes (yes, they do exist where applicants forget to change the school address or the head teacher's gender) but makes you focus on this one particular post. It goes back to a point made earlier that if you do not put everything into your application, its chances of failing soar.

As teachers we don't often write business letters ourselves, so if you are unsure on a format check out the next letter from your bank or some other institution where these things are important.

As to how you write your letter, it all becomes very personal. Try to stick to a logical format and hone it down over several drafts to a very lean and efficient document. Decide what the head will want and aim to meet those demands. Anything extraneous to this has to be considered very carefully and probably rejected. If the head doesn't want to know why tell him? This is really hard to do. You have worked hard to accumulate all this evidence so leaving it out seems very wonky indeed, but realize that if isn't relevant then it doesn't go in. If you have the space, try to bend the things you are most proud of into the letter, but if you force it you will generate more questions. This is not always a bad thing. A little intrigue encourages them to ask you in for interview.

If you don't mention some fundamental aspect of teaching, like A to C rates in your exam classes, but everything else appears spot-on, then most heads will rely on their instincts on the day and call you for interview. They understand that context is all important so do not be too worried about something you haven't managed to notch up yet.

Applicants for a first management role have a balance to strike. Appearing competent and dynamic is difficult on the page, so redraft with the reader in mind. They will need someone they can trust but have to realize that you are not the finished article. You will have to be trained and learn many aspects of the job, but the less of this it appears you need the better candidate you will come across as. So the correct attitude to strike must be competent without being cocky, willing to learn and to make decisions. Difficult stuff indeed.

What follows are two examples of letters that try to project ability and persuade the reader that the applicant is worth calling to interview. Have a read of both and think carefully which parts of the two styles you want to emulate the most.

Example 1

I would like to be considered for the post of French and German teacher as advertised in the *Times Educational Supplement* of 14th June.

I am in my third year of teaching both languages at Brighton High School, where I have found it rewarding contributing to an effective department and believe that I am ready to further my experience within a new environment. I am keen to work within an active and enthusiastic team where I can further my professional development and continue to produce stimulating ideas in the classroom as well as contribute to other aspects of school life.

At Brighton High School I have enjoyed being a valued member of a team and have made several contributions to Modern Languages by writing the departmental policies on Target Language and Differentiation; restructuring the German resources; creating a Modern Languages corner in the library; organizing European Cafés and increasing the use of the computers. I believe in the value of ICT in Modern Languages, not only for variety of delivery, but also for independent research, contact with native speakers and maintaining links with partner schools. Consequently, I am writing the departmental ICT policy and working towards whole-class use of computers.

I have taught A Level German since arriving at Brighton High School and it has been a consistently challenging yet rewarding experience. It is vital to be up to date, not only with the language but also with all the topics in the syllabus in order to be able to provide pupils with the necessary information and to be able to motivate and encourage them to carry out personal studies. With this in mind I took a group of sixth formers to Berlin, where they were able to carry out research and gain first-hand information for their coursework.

I believe it is essential to raise interest and awareness of the value of languages for both male and female pupils as far as future employment opportunities are concerned, particularly the wider European job market, and to improve links with other curriculum areas, e.g. Careers, Business and GNVQ. This can be accomplished in many ways but I think that the fundamental delivery of the curriculum must be stimulating in order to generate interest. I consider myself an organized and innovative practitioner with the enthusiasm to motivate pupils of all abilities to study languages and I am keen to promote the subject within the school, putting languages into the cross-curricular whole-school picture.

It is vital to instil a desire to learn and explore a subject, motivating pupils to want to increase their knowledge. Negotiating individual targets and giving appropriate rewards allows all pupils equal access to the curriculum and provides opportunities for students to see and take ownership of the progress they are making and thus be further motivated.

At Brighton High School I have been on the German exchange on two occasions, firstly as accompanying teacher and secondly as leader. I believe that the experience has given me further confidence in taking responsibility for groups of students and organizing activities. In addition, working with parents and staff in Germany and England provided me with the opportunity to increase my skills in working and liaising with colleagues.

As a member of the pastoral team I have worked actively to help members of my form achieve their potential and attain the highest standard of which they are capable, intellectually, socially and personally. The current system at Brighton allows me to develop this part of my daily practice and it is a role which I have thoroughly enjoyed and would be glad to continue at your high school.

I believe in taking an active role in the development of a school and while I appreciate that achieving success is one of the most significant goals of a pupil's education, I also feel that schools play an important part in the ideas of citizenship. As such I have been involved in the school council and have initiated a whole-school paper recycling programme, leading to tutor groups organizing and having responsibility for their environment. I am also chairperson of the staffroom committee and have enjoyed the opportunity to build good relationships with other members of staff and play an active role in improving the environment in which we work.

Extra-curricular activities are highly important and I consider it essential to be involved with the students in areas outside the classroom. I have accompanied Duke of Edinburgh trips to North Norfolk and to the Peaks assessing both Bronze and Silver qualifying expeditions. Furthermore I have accompanied three summer camping trips, which I had an instrumental role in organizing. I play the piano and flute and am a keen hockey player and would enjoy the opportunity to get involved in either of these as an extra-curricular activity.

Getting Promoted

I believe that I have the experience and enthusiasm to take an active role at Charleston High School and the determination to bring initiatives and ideas to assist in the development and continuing progress of the department and school. I look forward to having the opportunity to discuss these issues in more detail.

Yours sincerely

Example 2

I am writing to apply for the post of Head of History as advertised in the *Times Educational Supplement* of 17 June 2003.

Having joined Ipswich High School as a newly qualified teacher in 1999, I was promoted to the position of Assistant Head of History in 2002. I now feel that I have gained the necessary experience within my current post, and that I am ready for the challenge that leading a History department would give me.

During my time at Ipswich I have taught both History and PSHE at all Key Stages, helped to rewrite the schemes of work for my department, and have assisted in organizing History trips and fieldwork. I am currently making the final arrangements for a Sixth Form study visit to Northern France, planned for next month. I am a strong supporter of foreign visits, as I believe that they present students with the cultural and contextual benefits that we, at times, can not provide. They also serve to strengthen the relationship between pupils and staff.

In my present post I have gained valuable

experience in working effectively as a team, supporting and motivating colleagues in striving to raise achievement amongst students of History. I am training to be a team leader in my school's performance management system and have been responsible for the organization of paired observation within the Humanities faculty. I am of the opinion that watching other colleagues in the classroom can help to promote a continual development of good ideas and good practice, which in turn can result in the raising of standards and attainment amongst students. I am responsible for the setting of all students from Year 9 to 11, and for the monitoring of student assessment and performance in History and for all examination entries.

I have played a pivotal role in bringing about progressive change within the department, both in terms of embracing new concepts and strategies, and also in raising the profile of History throughout the curriculum, points both noted in our recent Ofsted inspection: 'History has a high profile in the school because it is actively promoted by an enthusiastic department.' I have made good use of value-added data as an effective aid to target individual pupils and, with colleagues, have continually worked towards each student maximizing his or her potential. With the recent introduction of new AS/A2 and GCSE specifications and the Key Stage 3 Strategy, which allow for increased opportunities for a wider range of ability, the status of History in schools has the potential to become even more prominent. I feel confident that I would be able to lead a team through all that these changes would entail.

Over the last three years, I have worked very closely with my Head of Faculty to gain experience in all aspects of running and managing a faculty. I have attended relevant courses, led by the Suffolk Advisory Service, aimed at increasing my knowledge and expertise. My experience has taught me that working together as a team is one of the key elements of successful management. I feel that I have the abilities to encourage and motivate others around me, so that as a team we can work towards the common goal of raising the achievement of pupils.

Outside of the classroom, I am keenly involved in extra-curricular activities. I have coached the school's U11 and U16 football teams, and hold KS3/4 coaching certificates. I also enjoy playing the clarinet and have done so in various school concerts and dramatic productions. I have also helped organize trips to Dunkirk and the Ardeche, all of which I feel contribute in some way to making the concept of school life a better experience for young people.

From my experiences as a pupil, I quickly learned to enjoy History, since my teachers were very enthusiastic and helpful. These are qualities that I have tried to emulate since I have been in the profession, and I thoroughly enjoy what is a demanding yet rewarding career. I feel that I have a lot to offer Bridlington High School and that I could make a valuable contribution to the life of the school. I would be delighted to attend should you wish to call me for interview.

Yours sincerely

Two very different ways to approach the same task. They show how even small things can be used to illustrate how suitable you are for the post. How much spouting of personal belief should be decided by considering what you are prepared to talk about at interview. Inclusion signifies that you are thinking about your practice but some consider it pretentious to mention the thoughts of eighteenth-century East European professors.

I am well aware that 'those who can, teach' and in no way do I doubt your abilities in anything, but get your letter checked before you send it. Do not settle for the closest person to hand either. For checking grammar and construction and all that stuff never underestimate your English department. They review this sort of thing all day and there is bound to be an unhostile one in there somewhere. If you are an English specialist ask somebody with a different discipline to read through for you. It is probable that most of the intended recipients will not be English teachers so it has to make sense and read well to everybody. Do not discount the need for the grammar to be perfect. It may be old fashioned but the target audience is still likely to be older than you and the requirements this brings have been discussed above.

Asking your friends and colleagues is an essential step, but acting on their advice is a matter of choice. Errors must be corrected but consider input on content very carefully. Can the change from your original script be justified? Let the person proposing the alteration convince you with a reasoned argument rather than just that it is what they think. This opens up the entire can of worms marked truth and honesty. You want the school to employ you because of who you are and might become, rather than on the quality of your English department.

Once your letter is posted

Obviously, waiting to see if you have succeeded is the main thing to preoccupy your thoughts, but at this point you must presume that they will call you for interview. Only that way can you have the right mindset established for the coming difficulties. After applying for two jobs at about the same time one of my potential Head teachers rang me out of the blue. Only because I had all my preparation on the table in front of me was I able to appear focused and talk knowledgeably and intelligently (-ish) about the position.

Keep the research going but bear in mind that, strong though the labour market is, there is a chance that you will not be called. It is not a waste of effort to keep working at your application while the school considers it. The work that you put in now will pay off at some point in the future.

Most information packs from schools will specify an interview date, so you can feel disappointed if you have not been called a week before it. But the reality is that many schools will have people cry off or get jobs beforehand, especially in the peak recruitment period of the first half of the summer term. Any application you make will be kept until the post is filled, sometimes even after the interview day because nobody who attended was considered good enough. Rather than incur the expense of readvertising many schools will change their criteria and sift through the applications again, so do not give up too quickly.

An 'informal visit' before you apply

Some schools offer you the opportunity to go and have a quick look round first. This is not a good idea under any circumstances. You will already have some idea of the school and by presenting yourself this early you might undermine all your good work. The school offers this so that it can refine its field for interview. Rather than rely on your letter of application they will now have a chance to form their own opinion. This gives everybody else an advantage over you. If there is something that will put you off it will be there on the day and you can withdraw but they have to invite you first.

These 'opportunities' tend to be after school too, so what can you learn about a school when there are no kids in it? Altogether wise to avoid.

Top Tips 3

1. Have your family or partner's backing.

2. Research potential schools before they advertise a job.

3. When a job you want comes up put everything you can into getting an interview.

4. Search out opinions but be careful of bias.

5. Be very informed about every school you apply to.

6. Observe the classical rules of presentation when applying.

7. Ensure your referees will write good reports on you.

8. Write a new letter for each job.

4

Preparing for Interview Day

Know your limitations and be content with them. Too much ambition results in promotion to a job you can't do.

Getting the call

When a letter finally does come through treat yourself to a night off marking, a bottle of wine (or a sensible alternative) and some serious thinking and planning. Sift through the details you are sent and make an educated guess about why they have been included. Much like the application pack, be wary of mutton dressed as lamb and overboard policy documents. However, details of why the vacancy arose, the make-up of the department and the school's own perceptions of its strengths can be invaluable.

This is not a time to fret and worry over details (there will be plenty of time to do that later), but a time to prepare yourself for the most overlooked question in these situations. Do you want the job?

The reason why this sometimes gets forgotten is because candidates get taken along in the excitement of opportunity. Do not allow this to happen to you. Keep a distanced and balanced view. Any promotion, and especially your first, is a stressful one so always bear in mind that at any point you can withdraw, even if it is because the post doesn't feel right. It might not be easy but these are relatively big steps you are taking so the consequences of not pulling out when the feeling is not right are much bigger than looking a bit of a wally on the day.

The chances are that having come this far you will stay on course and attend the interview. A list of typical components you might face will be dealt with later, but only after two overarching comments.

Whenever it becomes known that somebody is preparing to escape a school, a grizzled old-timer will take them off to one side and, with sincere warmth, tell them that the key to succeeding is 'To Be Yourself'. This is obviously and patently not true. If you were to be yourself you would not have to be polite to that creepy kid in Year 9, wouldn't wear a shirt and tie or smart shoes everyday and you would not spend your time discussing anything but football in moronic meetings. Work, schools and adult life in general have nothing to do with the 'real you', so why persevere with being yourself?

Take the opportunity to present somebody who is better than you are at the moment. Work at being better and you will get there. Piddling around being satisfied with what 'yourself' represents is a recipe for mediocrity and a sure-fire way to fail at getting promotion. That is why the grizzled old-timer is such a cynic; they are convinced that being themselves will be enough to set the world alight, so why work at improving? Don't fall into their make-do attitudes and condemn yourself to sitting in the same chair in the same staffroom in 20 years while saying to bright young things that the way to succeed is 'To Be Yourself'.

There is another cynic's cliché that you will always hear whenever your departure is possible. While it is normally meant with the best intentions, the phrase 'You don't want to go there ...' with accompanying sharp intakes of breath and teeth-sucking is another to be ignored. Make your own mind up. It does not matter when, just make sure that you, and only you, make up your mind. Singularity and clarity of thought are the must-have qualities all the way through the process.

What this translates to in a day-to-day context is a process of self evaluation and targeted self improvement. In an interview situation it means being flexible enough to sell the qualities you have that best meet the needs of the school you are aiming to join.

The other big issue at this point and throughout the whole interview process is not to be rushed or panicked. Interview is perhaps the most stressful aspect of teaching for many, but the ones who succeed tend to be the least perturbed. At all points along the way to your new job be calm. Do not confuse this with cool. Cool is something it is nice to have but by calm I mean appearing controlled enough to be professional but concerned enough to show you really want the job – uninterested is not the right image to project!

Before the interview

This is the time to do the donkey work so that the day goes smoothly. In no particular order, buy yourself a new shirt so that you feel confident, make sure your suit is pressed and your shoes are shiny (unless they are suede), organize a taxi and accommodation as soon as you can, have a map and a phone number of the school, set your work a couple of days before you go so you can leave school at a decent time the night before, get a haircut, work out how long it will take to get there, make sure you do not have a curry etc., etc. All mundane stuff but all needing organizing to make sure you arrive on the day in the best possible position.

The interviews at this level are frequently pre-dictable; a tour of the school, a mini interview with a senior manager, a formal interview with the head teacher and some other big cheeses. It is becoming increasingly common to set a middle management interviewee a task. Presentations are very popular (with the schools) but others have been asked to teach lessons, sit psychometric tests and bring portfolios of work. All these present their own difficulties, some of which you can prepare for others that you cannot.

Presentations

If you are asked to present on a topic as part of your interview try to think beyond the title. If, as I have been, you are asked to present on something that is so esoteric and theoretical as to be irrelevant to day-to-day teaching, ask yourself why? The chances are that the people listening will not be concerned with the title very much at all. Instead, they will be looking for some hidden agenda. It could be presence, ability to cope with pressure, how prepared you are or how you can think around a new problem. Of course, you must address the question but make sure that the message does not obscure the messenger – nobody has ever been given a job as a middle manager because of their views on whether continuity and progression are important.

Think about the audience sitting there with a check list, trying to tick off each attribute that they are seeking. Therefore this task presents all sorts of potential pitfalls. Of course you must aim to address as many of the unspoken requirements as you can, but don't get too caught up in trying to be everything to everyone. This is where any inside knowledge you have is very useful. Decide what the school wants, what you can supply and how your presentation is going to show that you are the right person for the job. If, after trying for inside information from friends and Ofsted and the material sent through, you have no way of knowing what the school is looking for, work at trying to project the qualities you would most want in a head of department. This fail safe attitude helps you choose the school as much as the school choosing you.

The school tour

I have tried to keep the anecdotes to a minimum so far but I am convinced that I once secured a job on the strength of how I behaved on the school tour. It was obvious that the head teacher was really pupil orientated and we were shown around by two prefects. As we went round and saw the usual highlights of the dining room and the sports fields my competition held us up by talking to staff about teacher trivia (you know, stuff that nobody ever cares about when they are not on interview, like what assessment criteria were being used and the arrangements for wet lunchtimes). This gave me the opportunity to speak with the kids showing us around. We are, after all, supposed to be interested in them above all else. Months later I was teaching one of them and we got talking about the day. He had been extensively questioned on each candidate and how they conducted themselves so, as the only one who had bothered to ask his opinions, I was given the best review. Obviously I am great (ha-ha) but I am sure that the prefect's testimony stood me in very good stead for the later stages.

Of course, you must talk to staff, but we are trying to get an edge by playing the system. When you are talking to staff do not ask them leading questions otherwise you will get biased answers. Stick to the polite and customary stuff and you will not go wrong.

On the tour, or indeed at any stage, do not forget that you are being evaluated. Have some questions prepared that are obvious to ask but not easily answered if you don't work there. Ask about the catchment area or the recent changes to the school day but do not fall into the trap of asking questions for question's sake. Let your rivals do that. There will be enough opportunities to speak with the head so don't overplay your hand too early. Remember that he or she will be forming an opinion of you as a person and boring, stupid questions will not show you off as the appointment of their dreams.

Portfolios

Providing a portfolio is often a black and white issue for teachers; they have one or they don't: This is sometimes because of who you are but most frequently because of what you teach. ICT, Technology and Art specialists often have a portfolio accumulating as routine, the rest do not and do not always have much they can show at short notice any way. The guidelines to keep to are keep it short and make sure the work is marked, very well ordered and genuinely worth showing off. Try to include what is currently cutting edge in your subject area but make sure that it won't put anybody's nose out of joint if they find out you are using it. Take it whether the interview asks for it or not and keep it in the car, waiting for the opportunity to show it off. I would particularly recommend photographs of kids in action – how child centred you will look if you show the kids on your side!

The school dinner

If most teachers are as busy as they say then few will be used to sitting down and having a formal lunch with colleagues. I am sure this is true for a thrusting young buck like yourself but it sometimes worth having a school dinner as practice for the big day.

Getting Promoted

It is really quite difficult to maintain polite and valid conversation while eating pizza, chips, salad, sausage and beans so don't even try. Have a small snack; overeating is very much frowned upon during a free lunch, and keep quiet while the other candidates try to say something sensible with a mouth full of sponge pudding. Let them make the mistakes.

I always have a sandwich. There is no knife and fork etiquette to be ignorant of, I eat fast and I am normally so nervous by lunch that I don't want the extra concerns of the flatulence that a big, fatty meal in a stressful situation will cause. (I can be quite a nice person, really.)

The staffroom

After the actual interview the situation that needs the most thought is the interminable hanging around. In some ways this is actually a good chance to read all those notices on the staffroom wall that they have in your school but you have never had the chance to read. You should make sure it does not become time to get nervous and goof things up in.

If you do spend your time reading the Union news letters and staff fantasy football tables then you are missing a chance to get a real insight into what the place is really like. Do not be put off by lots of notices about discipline or truancy. Of course they are not an ideal sign, but are they being dealt with? Is the pastoral system on the ball and the kids responding? Does the senior management team seem in control and proactive? Are the latest initiatives being taken up? Are minutes available?

Some schools hide details of training so that nobody realizes there is not any money for them to attend! Is there a clutter of dog-eared *TES*s on the dirty coffee table? Do the easy chairs have the buttock grooves worn in to them? Are the noticeboards covered in out-of-date notices or dynamic fresh ones about extra-curricular or staff social events?

The best time to be in the staffroom is at break and lunchtime. If there is a procession of moaning caffeine addicts then think carefully before continuing through the process. Is everybody over 50? If so, then life might be very tough for you as the youngest; everyone needs somebody to cry on/swear viciously at. What the teaching staff are like at your potential job is sometimes very underrated as a criterion for taking a job but life will seem much harder if you don't have a laugh or moan with somebody you like or can relate to.

Better still, don't stay in the staffroom, get out and about and see how a random sample of the school colours your judgement. You know your strengths and preferences, how will you shape up here? If there are lots of kids standing outside rooms do you have the disciplinary presence to make a difference? Remember that whatever the post promises it will count for little against a drop in your quality of life.

If you have free time at lunch take the time to see your new students at play. Find out if there is a nice atmosphere around the playground or whether little kids live in fear of the big kids. I have asked the lunchtime supervisors before but they are so browbeaten that it is very hard for them to say very much positive at all, no matter how nice the students are in the classroom.

So use the waiting time to confirm or confound your expectation rather than twiddle your thumbs. Not only does it give you more information but it gives you the appearance of a go-getting dynamic sort of person. Exactly the sort any decent school would want to employ.

A lesson

More and more schools are asking interviewees to teach a lesson on the day. There are all sorts of things that could go wrong but any decent school will keep these to a minimum. The kids will be willing, the time short and the expectation is to show competency rather than brilliance. Make sure that you have a learning objective even if you have to ring and ask for one. Similarly, try to have an idea about the lesson context; without either of these your job is much harder and it will speak volumes about the school if basics like this have not been thought through.

Think carefully about what strengths you can show in such a short time. If you are confident enough to use a new teaching method go for it, but do not increase the stress on yourself if the thought scares you silly. Be engaging without being overly familiar, have an activity lined up in case you finish early, remember all the theory etc., etc. It is just like an observation at college after all.

By the time the interview comes along you will have a very good idea of what sort of school you are in. You will also have used the opportunities, where they arise, to think long and hard about whether you want to be involved here too. All that research, effort and stress now comes down to should you continue or withdraw.

Do not put yourself or the interviewing panel through the trauma of interview and then withdraw. This is a waste of everybody's time. There is no point having the interview for experience's sake, that will just piss everybody off.

If you do decide that the post/school/department/ head is not for you, approach the nicest member of the senior management team you have met that day and politely and apologetically tell them the bad news. Make sure that the reason you give is because you don't fit rather than their school looks like a nightmare. Think about all those ways to dump your partner, like 'it's-not-you-it's-me'. Remember that heads do talk to each other so don't upset anybody.

If you decide to go for it, and having come this far it is likely that you will, be sure of one thing. If it appears that you are anything less than totally committed to the post then your chances of failing are hugely magnified.

If, during the day, certain problems that you do not consider too major appear then ask about them in interview. Use your eagerness and suitability for the job as a negotiating tool to get some assurances that things will receive people's attentions. It is a slightly risky thing to do but then how long are you prepared to wait for the perfect job with no problems whatsoever?

Top Tips 4

1. While your application is being considered keep working on it.

2. Make sure you want the job. Make your own mind up at every stage.

3. Work at projecting the person the school wants by stepping back and thinking.

4. Be organized and prepared.

5. Prepare to be constantly evaluated through the day so be dynamic, proactive and committed.

6. Make a conscious decision to continue or withdraw before interview.

5

The Interview Itself

When confronted by a difficult problem, you can solve it more easily by reducing it to the question, 'How would the Lone Ranger handle this?'

Everything that you have worked towards up until this point is distilled into the next hour. Excellent candidates that have been favourites since their letters of application arrived have lost the plot and the job within the first 10 minutes of interview. People have failed to get appointed because of their interview. Full stop. Period. End of story. So if someone tells you to just go in there and be yourself by relaxing and saying what comes into your head ignore them. They are spouting platitudes because they have nothing interesting to say.

Hopefully, on your letter of confirmation there will have been a mention of who will be interviewing you. If not someone will have let it slip during the day. Think about what each one will ask you. So if the deputy in charge of the curriculum is in there then expect questions about improving exam results. If there is a parent governor scheduled to appear then it is not too much of a leap to imagine that they will ask about the things parents are concerned about, such as failing teachers and homework.

Governors will often ask you about your life outside of school. They are on the panel to bring a little bit of the real world into schools. So expect questions about what you are most proud of or what your perfect day would be. Be honest but do not be stupid, remember the type of people you are talking to. If car jacking and absinthe are your thing I would recommend lying.

Whoever is in the room with you, there are several topics that I can guarantee will be brought up in a middle management interview. Part commonsense, part what ever is currently vogue, they will need some preparation.

Monitoring

There, I have said it. If there is one topic that will cause you more hassle than anything else during your management career it is monitoring the performance of your staff. You don't enjoy having it done to you, you won't enjoy doing it and it more often than not irritates the hell out of anybody who has it done to them. Monitoring is the proverbial can of worms but the bottom line is that there is no more effective way you can gauge performance.

This means you must be prepared to exemplify what experience you have of being the monitor, a rationale of why it is worthwhile and a plan of how you would put it into place. Your own personal feelings are redundant, it is an accepted truth in the twenty-first century school and you ignore it at your peril.

Focus on the positives but be prepared to be grilled on the negatives.

The failing teacher

As part of the fallout from the raising of standards in teaching in the UK, how middle managers deal with failing teachers has become a real burning issue. It will come up in interview because ensuring effective teaching and learning should be the main job of any manager in education and because it is simply the hardest thing in education management to deal with. Heads of year in particular are having to deal with this very thorny issue for the first time.

How you deal with it in interview is up to you but know that it will come up and that there is no shame in admitting that it is a difficult topic to solve effectively. Indeed, a gung-ho approach that does not recognize how utterly complex a problem it is would be wrong.

Using technology

On your tour of the school the state and status of information technology will have become evident. If technology college status is proudly displayed and there are banks of computers humming in every department then be sure to have an interesting example of using IT in your teaching. Be careful, however, if there is only one creaky suite of ancient machines not to dismiss the need to be prepared to talk about using the technology. It is probably because teachers are not using IT innovatively that the investment has not been made, but aim to enlighten them about this without being smug.

The form tutor's role

Whichever middle management role you are applying for, you will be asked about this. As an academic leader you will be expected to pull your weight pastorally and by defining a good form tutor you are setting the level of expectation. As a head of year you are defining an ethos which you will project on to your team of tutors. Either way be very prepared to impress with an answer that shows warmth, compassion and care.

What would you bring/why should we employ you?

Before answering, have prepared a whole raft of personal qualities you have the nerve to admit to owning while being careful not to be too arrogant. You know the sort of thing: enthusiasm, diligence, a new set of eyes, etc, etc., a question not so much about what you say but how you say it.

Dealing with complaints from students and parents about teachers in your department

This is a stinker and should be approached with caution. Schools have systems in place to deal with this sort of thing and of course you will not know what they are so you have little choice but to begin with an answer about following the school procedure. This shows you are aware of the expectations upon you to fit in to an organization. Any thorough interviewer will follow up with what you would do then. Have an answer ready that treats all the parties involved fairly.

How would you deal with ...

Much like the parental complaint above, this question is testing out how you would fit in to the ethos of the school. Be sure to reference that the internal procedures have to be followed but unfortunately beyond the most clichéd it is difficult to predict the situation that will be presented. This is an opportune moment to take your time and consider rather than jump in. Older people often view your dynamism as hot-headedness so a thoughtful approach will be noticed and appreciated.

Raising the profile of your year group/subject

Schools are increasingly reacting to the pressures of publicity and so profile raising is the new rock and roll for heads. You are in a great position because you know all about trying to find out about the place and you are a new set of eyes on the situation, but there is scope to prepare ahead with ideas about raising your year group's or department's profile. Think about open evenings and websites and the like.

There are plenty of other questions that can be asked and here are a summary of some of the areas I have heard or been asked, in no particular order:

- Questions about commitment/sincerity/personal qualities.

- The place of your subject in the curriculum and in the whole school.

- How can a good practioner be identified?

- What is the importance of your subject for particular ages and abilities?

- Approaches/philosophies to teaching.

- Questions about resources.

- The wider role of teachers.

- The wider role of the subject leader.

- Why do you want to teach here?

- How can you support your team of tutors/subject teachers?

What questions would you like to ask?

You must say something that is sensible or say no thank you: do not fall into the trap of asking something for the sake of asking it. You can prepare what you are going to ask or, more likely, your time in school will have brought something to your attention. You are quite within your rights to ask if money will be made available or if there is potential for you to acquire a whole-school role in time. Be careful not to be too aggressive or to be too keen to take on extra responsibility. The interviewing panel's first thought will be to make sure that your area will be improved and don't let them think that you will be distracted from your core task.

Conduct in the interview

It would not be unreasonable at this point to think that interviews are the proverbial piece of cake. So why is there serious consideration of banning them under the EC's Human Rights Charter? It can only be because of the pressure. While writing this I can recall the bowel-churning sensations that are endured during interview and it is this fear that is your biggest enemy.

The key preparation you must make is how to deal with the pressure. It is the one thing that you cannot predict. How you will react is the biggest unknown until you are put through it so develop some subtle displacement activities to gain control of yourself.

One place that pressure and nerves will peak is

obviously during the interview itself, but do not be surprised if the worst butterflies come while you are waiting to go in. Go for a walk, write your questions, go and talk to the secretaries, whatever – just do something other than sweat nervously in the staff-room.

Which brings up the most personal aspect of this whole book: if there is one tip I have to remember when I walk in to the dreaded interview room it is to ask if I can take my jacket off. Otherwise there is a good chance that I will spontaneously combust or drown in my own sweat before 15 minutes have passed. (Perhaps I shouldn't have mentioned that!)

Deal with the pressure in your own way. Have some stock answers prepared but don't be afraid to go with whatever is in your head at the time. Make sure that you tread carefully the thin line between assertive and aggressive, especially when being chased for an answer on a particular question, and do not be afraid to answer the trickiest questions with 'I would have to ask a senior member of staff'. Nobody expects you to be the finished article and would much rather that you did come to them than bodge it right up.

You need to remember to exhibit the right body language (keen), give lots of eye contact to the person asking the questions and hope for heaps and heaps of good luck. I have avoided chance because interviews are about being really positive but sometimes you have to chalk up an interview day to experience. I was once turned down for a first appointment because I was too keen. Can you think of a less valid reason?

Top Tips 5

1. Be prepared.

2. Don't be afraid to finish speaking.

3. Know the answers to the predictable questions before you go into the interview.

4. Think up questions to ask before and during the day.

5. Think about your body language and eye contact.

6. Prepare to deal with nerves.

6

Aiming for Promotion in Your Existing School

You don't have to be mad to work here, but you do have to be on time, well presented, a team player, customer-service focused and sober!!

There are significant differences in the approach required depending on whether you wish to be promoted internally or externally. Much of the advice above is pertinent to both, but each situation has advantages and disadvantages.

For promotion within your current school, explicit foundations can be laid down at several key moments in the ordinary school year but the biggest benefit of working for promotion in-house is that you know the job you want. This requires a certain degree of realism from you about what you are capable of and who is likely to leave which posts, but be very clear which jobs you would be prepared to do and which you would not.

Be certain too that the kids and the staff would be receptive to you and your new status. As previously discussed, promotion changes everybody's perception of you; can you take the hassle without resorting to the time-honoured cliché 'Do you know who I am?' (This has been personally witnessed by the author and the less said about the speaker the better.)

A good place to start in your quest is in the Performance Management process. You have to do it, so it might as well be utilized fully. It does, of course, depend very much on who your interview is with, but be bold. The whole process is about you and your professional development so state your objectives. I wouldn't couch it as 'I want your job' but there is no need to hide your ambition. Once you have the concept out in the open devise your targets around getting promoted. Discuss what needs doing in the department, how you could help the pastoral system or what you need to do to assemble the appropriate experience. This is not a time to do as you are told but an opportunity to raise awareness of, and progress towards, your first promotion.

I would hope that this far into the process the need for you to be seen to be a dynamic team player does not need spelling out. Everything that applied above to building up your CV applies doubly in this situation. Show dedication to the institution and it will greatly aid your cause.

But be prepared for everything being a double-edged sword. At interview you may well have an insight in to the workings of the school but that might make it harder to see the changes that need to be made. You will know of the strengths and weaknesses of the team you are inheriting but being friends with them might make the tough decisions even tougher.

That said, it is probably easier to be promoted internally because you do not have the stress of starting a new school, with all that entails, and you do not have to start a new relationship with your head teacher.

Top Tips 6

1. Know which jobs you want.

2. Fully utilize the Performance Management system.

3. Make sure that everyone knows how proficient and effective you are.

4. Try to grow into roles over time to keep your evidence base growing.

7

How to Impress in Your First Post of Responsibility

There's no 'I' in 'team'. But then there's no 'I' in 'useless smug colleague', either. And there's four in 'platitude-quoting idiot'. Go figure.

Once you have been successful at interview the hard work starts again. While you work your contractual notice at your current school do not take your foot off the pedal too much. Stay keen and hard-working so that you leave positive memories with the staff there. Who knows who will ask them about you next time you apply for a job?

There is bound to be some sort of holiday between leaving one job and starting another and it is important that you use it fully. Go away somewhere warm; decorate your house; whatever you decide make sure that you switch off from school completely as much as is practical. For instance, there is no need for you to take marking away with you and to post it back when it is done. Some schools will ask you to do this but get it done while turning up to work there if given a reasonable time span to complete. If they don't give you the time they cannot want you to do it!

Starting a new school is one of the most stressful things in teaching. All the hard work you have put in to get the students on-side has to begin again. There are a whole new set of procedures to learn and a whole new set of staff to get to know. Starting is made even more difficult when you have responsibility too. From the start people will be bringing problems to you so spend a lot of time thinking how you will react to all foreseeable problems before you start.

There are also some more theoretical questions to pose yourself. Go over your interview day and try to work out what it is you have been employed to do beyond a simple job description. Does your area have to be dragged kicking and screaming into the twenty-first century? Is there a member of staff who upsets everybody or is ineffective? The other questions you must prepare for are 'Who is it important to impress?' and 'Who can you impress?'

This comes across as very mercenary but I am assuming that this first post is a stepping stone to other things. In no way am I advocating doing a bad or slapdash job. The best way to impress is to do an excellent job but, as you will find out, middle management is very hard work and some people need to know that there is a way out or they go mad!

Away from the pressure of interview you now need to be the manager you aspired to be when you began to look for promotion. Remember that it is ok to be different provided that there is a reason for it. Changing the exam specification is fine as long as there is logic behind your decision. Most teachers have undergone change for change's sake plenty of times before, so there are few positives to be gained from doing it to them again.

The best bit about seeking promotion now is that the opportunities to impress are thrust upon you rather than you having to seek them out.

Exam results

Whether you are a head of year or department the one thing that you can guarantee that you will be held accountable for are exam results. Particularly as a subject leader, pass rates and residuals will haunt you so get to grips early on. Everybody will be asked to explain their respective area's performance so get ahead of the game and have a detailed analysis ready so that it does not have to be rushed. Make sure that you analyse performance by gender, performance with regard to any target grades set, how each individual teacher's classes performed and produce a meaningful residual for each student and member of staff. This gives a statistical look at what happened, so complete the picture by taking the time to speak with each teacher individually.

Think about the messages that will send out; you are on the ball, you know what is going on, individuals are going to be asked to explain themselves and so on. But if people have excuses listen to them and judge their validity. Use these dialogues to spot the holes in the system already in place and to guide your thinking. At each point of dialogue ask people for their opinions, it is quite likely that they will have more experience than you and if they do not, think back to how much you would have liked to have been involved in their position.

Getting Promoted

All this leads rather nicely into your first department or year team meeting. It focuses everybody on your main ambition of raising achievement which is very difficult for old cynics to argue as unimportant. At the very least they will need it to keep moving through the post-threshold scale.

Inspection, internal and external

Another fact of your new life will be inspection by various people at various times. Take them all very seriously and remember that you now have the power to influence what happens. Particularly during in-house evaluations you should take every opportunity to set the agenda bearing in mind that teaching and learning must be at the top of everyone's list.

If you are short of ideas then go back to your exam analysis and to previous inspection action plans, but it is more than likely that you will have a pretty shrewd idea in your own mind. Do not be too wary of hiding some objectives away in there too. If your team is a little hostile to certain changes engineer it so that the inspection team states these are to be put in place, then you will have to do them.

It is important that you soon realize that there are pressures on you above and beyond your job description. These become apparent from the start but inspection is a time when they come to the fore. People react very differently to the prospect of being evaluated. Some will become very nervous, others belligerent, others aggressive; it's your job to keep everyone on an even keel and get them to be as useful as possible, but remember that the person who comes out worst if they perform below expectation is the individual themselves so a poor lesson observation always comes in handy later as a stick to beat them with.

Meetings

Now that you are somebody in the school you will have a lot of different meetings to go to and several offers to attend some more. My advice is to say no to every meeting that is optional so that you have a chance to catch your breath, but when you have to go, realize the expectation upon you. Your head will expect you to do your best for the school, and therefore by extension, he and your staff will expect you to do your best for your area. These two do not always mean the same thing, on top of which there is a massive expectation that you will contribute your opinions in an intelligent and reasonable way. So already you are being pulled in many directions with little hope of pleasing all of the people all of the time. Welcome to middle management!

Before entering the meeting consider the agenda and how it will impact upon your area, and if it is important, use the meeting to make sure that everyone knows your opinion and reasons. However, everything said above about meetings and what the characteristics of the decision makers will be are still very relevant and keeping your mouth shut in your new role will only take you so far.

Something else that you will be expected to do a

lot more of is run meetings with your team. Never underestimate the value of writing the agenda for your meeting: it is the key to effectiveness and you dictate the length and the pace of the session. There is a lot of valuable advice about meetings in lots of places but the basics for you to decide are; how many items, how big a scope there is for discussion and how to focus discussion. Work hard to put as much information down on paper before the meeting as possible so that discussion and clarification can take place if necessary.

The biggest headache for young managers learning their trade is Any Other Business because it opens the meeting beyond their remit. Teachers are sometimes poor at realizing that their meeting will not set national policy so sometimes the meeting takes a turn for the worst when massive problems are not solved there and then. I have been in meetings where there is no AOB, where it comes first and where it comes last.

What works for you depends on who you have in your team but I would speak against no AOB at all. Meetings are about communication and if you stop people from participating then they will become frustrated and your meeting will therefore become less effective. It has also become trendy for meeting leaders to provide refreshments or organize a rota for other people to do this. Personally, I think it is a bit odd but if you think it will build your team then it must be all right.

Make sure that you do not take the minutes in a meeting you are trying to use positively. It is impossible to do it fairly in retrospect so get somebody to write for you as you go along and the office to type up. A positive step is to use action points so everyone is very clear what they are expected to do and when they are expected to do it by.

Monitoring

It was mentioned earlier that monitoring is the new black as far as teaching is concerned. After several years of focusing on teaching and how to improve the effectiveness of teachers, there is now a shift of focus towards learning. What you have to decide is what is important in your school, how it can be observed and how you project these values to your staff.

There are lots of ways to do this, none of which is easy. You can elect to drip the philosophy in gradually or go for a groundbreaking, dawn-of-a-new-age presentation. It is very much a personal decision, and that is the joy and the frustration of your new role. There are at least a dozen valid ways to do any task and you will never really know beforehand if you have chosen the right one.

I would hope that by this stage you have had some experience of observing other teachers. It is nerve-racking because at some point there will be a lesson to criticize and even grade as unsatisfactory. Hopefully, it will not be your first one so, to ensure that it is not, ask a friend if you can monitor them first. Another thing to do before putting your observation skills in public is to decide on a method of recording.

There seem to be two camps: one of writing everything that happens down and another of making a few notes about the key issues as they come to mind. You know your staff and so make a decision about what they will appreciate most. Some will be intimidated by you scribbling for an hour and others will want every point you make to backed up with an incident in the lesson. It is not just about lessons either. Marking and assessment need supervising, even if it just to say that you have done so, and reports need looking at too.

With all these monitoring issues the best advice I have for you is get started as soon as you can. The longer after your arrival you leave it the more difficult it will be to implement them. Arrive with a scheme and a pro forma to look at books as if it the most natural thing in the world: people will expect change from a new manager so live up to those expectations. If you try to change them later on they will perceive it as you reacting to their failings – and probably rightly so, but think about what it will do to morale and who would you rather work with: somebody who likes you or somebody who does not. Trust me, the former is much easier.

Monitoring other teachers is a tough thing to do so take things slowly and carefully. It is a very powerful tool for change and for progress so treat it delicately because if handled badly it can ruin a whole department. Similarly, don't try to do too much. Looking at other people's work is very time consuming so don't set yourself too high a target and make sure that you feedback to people. It does not matter too much how you do it, although people like to have it written down in today's post-threshold world, but make sure you say something positive at some point.

How to Impress in Your First Post of Responsibility

It has already been mentioned that you don't just have a new job, you have a role. If that sounds a little pretentious, and it should, think carefully before dismissing it. You have people looking to you for a lead, people expecting you to set standards and raise achievement, people have invested their faith in you to make their school a better one and some others are depending on you to get them the very best results they are capable of. And I know you had all these pressures before but now they are on a bigger scale. Instead of a form group, it is a year group. Instead of your GCSE class, it is every class in your subject area.

Once you have accepted that is indeed a role and not just a job, think about how you should carry yourself around the school and the most important aspect of that is how you interact with all the different people you now have different relationships with.

The head

How you deal with your head teacher is your business, but realize how integral she is to your future. She needs to produce good results from the kids with the minimum of fuss. Any amount of trouble you cause will still infringe upon her precious time, no matter how magnanimous she is at the time. Of course she wants to talk to you about how things are going, so don't hide away, but she does not want to know every detail. Always leave the impression of competency, even if that means that you had to ask for help. A little honesty about not knowing what to do is far preferable to a great big balls up.

Support staff

With the changes in teachers' working conditions in full swing, support staff are very important and becoming even more so. A lot of established middle and senior mangers are finding that working with support staff presents a new set of problems. They have a different motivation to teaching staff and require work to be structured in a different way too. Some people are getting in to all sorts of muddles because they have failed to grasp the core premise that these people are not less worthy because they are not teachers. Talk to them; let them share in the decision making, value them.

Classroom support assistants, for instance, have a really tough job for not very much money at all. Don't moan to them about whether it is the Caribbean or the Maldives this winter, be sympathetic. Talk to them about individuals that they work with who are causing you problems; they will know what works and when to use it. Some teachers dismiss the CSA with the rest of the class, how demeaning must that be for them?! When you do not need them any more say thank you and see you next time. Then you let them avoid the crush in the corridor or the scrum at the gate and they will be grateful and they will tell everyone who asks what a nice person you are and then the other support staff will go that extra mile for you when you are desperate. Hardly rocket science but it needs thinking about because if you don't and you are caught up in the inevitable rush of a school day then you will abuse these people's natural kindness and generosity, which will create all sorts of problems for the future.

Secretarial staff and caretakers are similar. They are not, as legend would have it, the most important members of staff but they deserve to be treated well and most teachers do not do that. It might be the only time that day you have asked for a letter to be typed in 20 minutes or to get the particularly green sick off the floor, but it is probably not the first time they have been asked. Be human with them and you, sad though it is to admit it, are a step ahead of your colleagues who have a very medieval attitude to the hierarchy of the school. Exploit the other staff's pretensions to grandeur and you will get a much better service from the support staff and sleep easily at night!

Your team

One key indicator, as opposed to decider, of your performance as a manager is the effectiveness of your team. Every group of teachers is unique and so once again it will be up to you to bind them into the best possible unit. That might mean that they work loosely connected or very tightly, that hardly matters; what matters is that they are a group prepared to change for the better and that produces the best education for the kids at your school.

Students

In practical terms the decider of your effectiveness as a middle manager are the students your department

Getting Promoted

teaches. Are they engaged and enjoying your subject? Do they feel wanted and cared for in your pastoral system? It is these sorts of things that you will be measured on professionally for years to come. Some are easy to spot and others have to be implied but still need to be considered.

The challenge that you face is not only how to measure them (and I do not mean to a decimal point), but which to look at in the first place. Do not be afraid to experiment because it will stand you in good stead later on. Try student forums and chats in the corridor, questions during covers and formal evaluations during lessons.

Heads of year face the biggest challenges here because too often their work is dominated by exactly the sort of child who will not have a very positive impression of them and much of their work is short-term fire-fighting. Try not to act in a vacuum and find feedback where you can by asking for peer comment. Sit down with somebody you trust or admire and ask them how they think you are doing. Take their advice as it is meant, i.e. positively.

I look back at this section rather embarrassed that I am so fixated about exam results. Of course there are other aspects of school life that are important, and better people than me have listed them, but there is only one that your head teacher will be able to explicitly measure and hold you accountable. Sorry, but it is a hard truth.

Top Tips 7

1. Make sure the school you are leaving has positive memories of you.

2. Use your holidays to relax.

3. Work out what you are being employed to do and make sure you do it.

4. Use everyday occurrences to build your evidence base.

5. Be conscious of the messages you send out, explicit or implied.

6. Make meetings and monitoring work effectively for you.

7. Deal with everybody at school professionally.

8

How to Get Your Second Promotion

Accept that some days you are the pigeon, and some days you are the statue.

I sincerely hope that your first taste of management leaves you wanting more. If so, give yourself a while to feel comfortable as a team leader then start the evidence-gathering process again. Go through the processes outlined above and put just the same amount of thought and dedication into applying for the next job. Do not be afraid to move sideways in order to gain experience and evidence of doing all the tough stuff that head teachers want their managers to be doing.

Also take care to try and introduce good practice that you have seen in your previous schools at the appropriate times but do it in a way that does not put people's backs up. Nobody likes the implicit message that you have come to their school to spread good news to the unwashed masses!

It is not too difficult to sit down with your line manager and draw up a checklist of things to achieve in one or two years that would prepare you for the next rung of the ladder. Make your career the centre piece of performance management interviews so that you broaden your role, provided that your department is doing well, and work hard to do a really good job of anything entrusted to you.

One valuable experience you must get as soon as possible is a whole-school role. This is bound to be really boring (that is why you are doing it and nobody else wanted it), and quite stuffy, but it will raise your profile enormously in the school (hopefully, because you got it right!). The thing you will notice straight away with whole-school issues is that things take so much longer. Rather than a quick meeting and a nod of heads, whole-school issues seem to need an eternity of paper chasing, taking back to departments and senior teacher meetings to get anywhere. Of course it is frustrating but the reason you are doing it is to get used to it for the future. Do not lose heart: it will finish sometime.

While your career thrusts forward do not forget your prime responsibilities to your department and to your kids. Too many aspirants forget these fundamentals in the buzz of writing the Year 12 Mock timetable or drawing up the policy on assessment in primary liaison. It is important that you continue to set high standards and keep your subject knowledge evolving – after all, you receive the vast bulk of your money for teaching and it will come in handy at the next interview if you can demonstrate what a great teacher you still are.

The really serious and committed career teachers are now studying at the weekends for formal qualification such as MAs and the array from the National College for School Leadership. If you can find the time they are highly recommended but if not try to keep abreast of their excellent publications.

How to Get Your Second Promotion

Below is included another example of the sort of letter you might be able to write when the second step in middle management is close.

Example 1

I am writing in response to your advertisement in the *Times Educational Supplement* on 22nd February this year asking for applications for the post of Head of Humanities.

I have been Head of Geography (Second in Faculty) at Stoney Bridge High School since September 2000 and during that time an already very good department has made improvements in results, expectations and delivery. Prior to that I was Head of Geography at Trumpton High School. Over the two years I was in the post, Geography made significant improvements and became one of the highest achieving subject areas in the school. At Stoney Bridge, Geography is a core subject to GCSE and one of the most popular A level subjects. Consequently, this year around 1500 students have studied the subject. Our results at the end of all key stages are well above the national average. For example, the A*-C rate for GCSE Geography is 69 per cent. Of particular pride to the department is the fact that boys achieve a better pass rate than girls, but only by 1 per cent. We have followed a determined strategy to support and encourage boys, particularly at the C-D borderline. I am particularly proud that these changes have the desired effect.

During October 2000 Ofsted inspected Stoney Bridge and reported that 'the department is enthusiastically led and well managed' and that 'the teachers combine

---

to form a most effective team … with the commitment and capacity to achieve further improvements'. In my second year as Head of Geography at Trumpton, Ofsted recognized 'significant strengths … in the management of Geography', that 'the subject is well managed by an enthusiastic head of department' and that there was 'good quality teaching in KS4 because of management, planning and resourcing'.

In my role as Second in Humanities I have particular responsibility for the development of ICT, the teaching environment, resources and discipline. I have included within this giving Inset on thinking skills and teaching with the Internet. A significant strand of development has been the improvement of Geography teaching by non-specialists through adapting schemes of work, simplifying assessment packages and updating resources to raise standards of graphicacy and differentiation.

Geography at Stoney Bridge is recognized nationally. Since my appointment the high standards of achievement have been built upon by using the strengths of the team to reflect and modify every aspect of our practice. There is more use of ICT, more monitoring of work, more enquiry-based lessons, less reliance on worksheets and an increase in the amount of local fieldwork. An already very good department is evolving into an excellent one.

The whole-school issue that I have responsibility for is to publicize the concept of Stoney Bridge's Sports College status to our community. The message that the whole school will benefit has been put across through assemblies, newsletters and by introducing the concept of sport and leisure as a vehicle for learning outside of the PE curriculum. A strand I have introduced to this is to greatly increase the number of sports-related work experience placements. Something I have also enjoyed building up within the PE facility has been the U14 Basketball team, who are now in the district final. I would be very keen to become involved with extra-curricular sport at Royston Vasey.

Another area I have been keen to develop is my own Geography teaching and knowledge. To increase my effectiveness I have been Assistant Examiner for five years, each time being graded as an excellent marker. I am convinced that my students and the members of my team benefit from my participation 'behind the scenes' in the form of better results. Earlier this year *GeoNews* published an article I had written and the County Adviser has seconded me to write fieldwork for the National Trust.

I was glad to see the emphasis placed on the role of the form tutor in the job description since it is something I take seriously and would look forward to continuing at Royston Vasey. It has been pleasing to see my difficult Year 11 form exceeding everybody else's expectations. I enjoy the opportunity to work with students outside the classroom and, to this end, I mentor two disaffected boys in Years 9 and 11. Both have made good progress due in some part to being able to talk their problems through and by having their achievements recognized.

I see my role as Head of Department as both facilitator and leader of teaching and learning. At Stoney Bridge this has meant developing a more open and supportive atmosphere between colleagues in which we are able to pool ideas, strategies and resources to work towards the common goal of higher student attainment. In addition, I have put new emphasis on students' learning and established the ethos of innovation in a supportive environment.

Getting Promoted

At Key Stage 3, Humanities teaching should be concerned with equipping students with the skills required to succeed at GCSE. It should establish a curiosity for explanation that extends the students' interest in issues of importance at all scales, particularly those pertinent to their lives. As such, it is ideally placed to continue to deliver many of the aspects of citizenship. One of the great strengths of Humanities is that it allows students of all abilities, particularly at the extremes of ability, to succeed because its basis in reality gives it credibility and relevance.

At Key Stage 4 teaching is primarily about maximizing the achievement of the student in formal examinations and as assessment becomes increasingly skills orientated, good teaching will become even more important. Part of the Head of Faculty's role must be to facilitate that outcome. A student's ability to implement an enquiry based approach is becoming ever more essential. Teaching should be engaging and stimulating with frequent reference to issues and places that the student can relate to. To this end, fieldwork has an important part to play in encouraging and including pupils in the learning process and it is a vital component of enquiry based learning and one of the fundamental tenets of student enjoyment.

This post offers me an excellent opportunity to broaden my experience as a teacher and as a manager in a different school environment and a successful faculty. I have the experience and enthusiasm to take an active role at Royston Vasey and the determination to ensure the continuing progress of the faculty and school.

I look forward to having the opportunity to discuss these issues in more detail.

Yours sincerely

This letter aims to put forward all the progress made since the applicant's last appointment in the best possible way. Some of the achievements mentioned are quite run of the mill but are not treated any more lightly because of it. Conversely, others are quite uncommon but nothing too much is made of them. The main job that the writer is being employed to carry out is, after all, to teach, and it would be easy to argue that the candidate includes too much and is over-qualified.

Which is exactly the point of everything that has gone before. Put yourself in a position where they cannot fail to see that you are the right person for the job. It is not over qualification, merely insurance against disappointment. Help the school you want to work at by making their tough decisions easy.

Top Tips 8

1. Rebuild your experience base to show you are a capable, useful and dynamic manager.

2. Keep doing the basics really well.

3. Acquire a whole-school role of substance.

4. Be patient trying to implement anything at a new, bigger scale.

5. Consider taking an external qualification.

Conclusion

The theory of promotion is simple. If you are good at your job and can present yourself well then advancing up the pay scale should be a breeze. However, like most things, it is never as easy as first thought. Nobody should be under any illusions that being an effective teacher is easy and so will not be surprised that the job of middle management is nearly as difficult.

If you succeed in your endeavours then life will be both tougher and easier. You will be stretched further and further but will have less of the nitty-gritty of teaching day in, day out to contend with.

You must never forget your experiences in the classroom. Personal philosophies are fine, but always remember that your core responsibilities are to the staff in your area, to your head teacher and to the children. There is no excuse to forsake any of these in pursuit of your personal goals. Indeed, it is difficult to imagine how anyone could sustainably advance very far without considering all of these groups.

The final issue to address is keep going. There are a host of valid reasons why you didn't get that job but as many why you will get the next one. Promotion is not an exact science and there are plenty of incalculable variables so if you do fail, do not be too harsh on yourself. Have a night out and start again tomorrow. Good luck!